Jason Mead

It Was Good While It Lasted

The autobiography of a child who became a victim of Jimmy Savile OBE

Copyright © 2021 All Rights Reserved.

It Was Good While It Lasted

Copyright © 2021 All Rights Reserved.

Table of contents

Chapter   **Page**

Table of contents   3
Forward   5
About the author   7
My childhood years   9
Groomed and assaulted in 1972   13
The consequences of abuse on my life   19
Finally reporting my abuser in 2012   27
Taking stock & managing the fallout   33
Invitation to meet the Speaking Out inquiry   37
Speaking Out – was not about listening to victims!   43
Victim status denied   47
Getting my MP involved   51
The Parliamentary Ombudsman   55
Ray Galloway, the Speaking Out team   61
CICA confirm victim status with compensation   71
Psychiatric care – at last   73
Ombudsman's second meeting year three   75
DOH pays more in legal fees than compensation   79
The ombudsman's decision   83
File sent to IICSA   85
Jeremy Hunt MP Statement   87
Missed Opportunity   89

It Was Good While It Lasted

Copyright © 2021 All Rights Reserved.

Forward

This is the true story of a twelve-year-old boy who was groomed and abused by Jimmy Savile in the Leeds General Infirmary in 1972, assaulted in his car and later witnessed him abuse a dead woman at the same hospital.

The autobiography provides details of the abuse and the consequences it had upon the life of the author.

Eventually, in 2012, following television documentaries detailing other victim's abuse at the hands of Savile, the author plucked up the courage to tell the police.

This is the story of how the author was mis treated by the police, solicitors, Speaking Out inquiry team, the Parliamentary and Health Service Ombudsman and the DOH legal department and the author is certain he was not the only victim selected for similar treatment.

Despite Jeremy Hunt stating in Parliament that the victims had been ignored and must be believed, he did not mean it, as this was not what happened.

It is the authors opinion that, as the vast machine employed to protect the NHS/DOH Parliament etc. from the fall out emanating from the Savile scandal rolled forward, it crushed the very people who it was supposed to listen to and learn from.

It is the authors opinion that as a result, others failed to come forward, resulting in the inevitable 2020 headline stories of another Savile like abuser, in the NHS, who has again been free to abuse unchallenged for decades.

About the author

The author wishes to remain anonymous as his family are unaware, he is a victim of Savile, hence as is common the author has taken a pen name, Jason Mead.

This autobiography details the way in which Savile groomed his victims, then abused them and subsequently dropped them when he had taken what he wanted, he left all his victims feeling that they were the only one, and due to his fame, no one would ever believe them, and he was right for many.

Out of 589 witnesses, 450 of which alleged abuse by Savile, the author, as far as he knows was the only victim to witness him abuse a dead person in an NHS hospital.

This autobiography is a true story. It names those public figures and organisations who were involved both at the time, and since the author reported the historical abuse to the police in 2012.

Full documentary evidence to back up every statement in the autobiography is archived both with the Parliamentary ombudsman and IICSA. In addition, the police, solicitors, Speaking Out inquiry team, Local MP and DOH legal team have the documents archived which refer to their parts in this story.

To preserve his sanity, the author destroyed all documents he held following the final determination from the Parliamentary Ombudsman, hence the author cannot copy and paste the text from original documents. However, the facts and sequence of events relayed in the autobiography are correct, to the best of his recollection.

It Was Good While It Lasted

Chapter 1

My childhood years

I am the eldest child of a large family, born to parents who met through their religion, and followed to the letter the traditional family values of the day.

This meant my mother, an Oxbridge level student with a professional career, sacrificing this because the man of the household was deemed to be the breadwinner in a family.

My father, a skilled tradesman in an outdated and no longer wanted profession, earned so little that we lived as poor as church mice.

My parents were of the opinion that in all things, God would provide. To an extent this was true, on several occasions the whole family were invited to dinner, quite an invitation for such a large family.

On one such occasion, I had no shoes or trousers having worn holes in both, after dinner the host said as we were leaving, there are some bags of clothes in the hall our kids have grown out of, please take them. The bags contained several pairs of shoes, two of which fitted me along with trousers, socks, shirts etc. some of which were a bit large but at least I could go to school the following day.

My parents attended church on Sunday, prayer meetings mid-week and counted many Christians among their friends.

They tithed their income giving a percentage of everything they earned to the Christian organisations they supported, which must have been hard to do when they had no food in the house and no clothes for their children.

The house we lived in was a Victorian four-bedroom terrace in a poor area of the city, it was heated by coal fires, there were two attic rooms which were not insulated; hence they were overwhelmingly hot in summer and utterly freezing in winter, they provided a room for all the boys, and another room for the girls. Another bedroom was taken for my parents and the largest bedroom at the front of the house was let to students who paid rent.

Growing up, we were isolated from many of the commonplace things families now expect, we had no radio or TV, no car and never had a meal out in a restaurant. A real treat would be to have fish and chips in newspaper once or sometimes twice a year.

What we did have though was religion, in my opinion too much religion. The constant presence was palpable in the home, blaspheming was utterly forbidden, bible readings were most days, prayers before bed were the norm, grace was always said before eating and even our holidays were planned around religious events.

At the age of eleven, I was to start at a local C of E secondary school, my mother was advised that our family would qualify for free school meals and uniform.

I went into town with my mother to Rawcliffe's, the school uniform outfitters. On arrival, a slimy salesman eager for more school uniform sales commission, fawned all over me, rubbing my shoulders and measuring my size.

What school will sir be attending, he asked and then dived into the stockroom re appearing minutes later with shoes, socks, two pairs of black trousers, five white cotton shirts, school tie, v neck long sleeved jumper, school blazer and cap all in the school colours, the blazer and cap were fitted with the school badge.

I was asked to stand on a low stool, stripped to my underpants and dressed in the uniform then shown myself in a mirror, it was a new experience for me as I had as far back as I could recall, never had clothes like this before.

Then came the bombshell, my mother produced the free uniform vouchers at the till. Seconds later the uniform was stripped from me and returned to the storeroom, when the salesman returned, he had with him two pairs of poor-quality crimplene trousers, two nylon shirts and a blazer which looked like it had been fashioned from cardboard.

Dressing me in this "free" low grade school uniform, he explained that this was the uniform provided for the voucher scheme, he went on to say that the tie, jumper, and cap were all extras and needed to be purchased separately as these were not included with the vouchers.

My mother took the items covered by the vouchers, and we left the store. I believe my grandparents returned later to purchase the jumper, tie, and cap as I would need these to be dressed in the school uniform.

Arriving on my first day I stood out from the crowd in my "free" uniform, there were just over a hundred new starters and I estimate eleven were wearing the same uniform I had on.

At lunchtime, I was separated from my peers in the free school dinner que. This que was only permitted to move forward after every other child had been served, so we stood for over forty minutes in the rain, in our poor-quality uniforms, seen by the whole school, when we were being served, chants of losers, losers were made by the fee-paying pupils, this was due to there not being enough food left to provide us with a choice.

I was a target for bullying, in my first two years, the police were called to the school three times to interview bullies for various serious assaults.

Chapter 2

Groomed and assaulted in 1972

At this time, my sister, who was two years younger than myself, was hospitalised in Leeds General Infirmary. My parents visited every day and on one occasion they took me with them, sitting around the bed with the curtains drawn closed we chatted for a while, then the consultant and his entourage arrived, they were pleased to see my parents and wanted to have a meeting with them, I remained with my sister and they all left into a side room on the ward.

A few seconds later, a strange, tall gentleman with white hair peeped around the closed curtain, seeing we were alone, he walked in and started to chat to us, he was wearing a white doctors coat and stethoscope, but had brightly coloured trousers underneath and gold shoes. He was carrying a box of Kentucky Fried Chicken, he climbed onto the bed next to my sister, unsure who he was, or what he wanted, we expressed caution however he was funny and friendly.

He was sorry my sister was in hospital and pretended to listen to my her chest and abdomen with the stethoscope. He then offered us both a piece of chicken from the box, as we started to eat, we agreed, we had never tasted food like this before. We asked where he had bought the chicken and he described the local Kentucky Chicken shop; we both knew where it was, and I went on to say that the best conker trees I knew were near the shop.

He started to speak to us about what our hobbies and interests were, mine at the time was collecting conkers, he said he would like to go with me, and I recollect thinking he would be able to reach the ones I could not. He asked if I knew where the nurses lived, and I replied in houses. He asked if I wanted to go with him to see where the nurses lived here in the hospital and I replied that I thought they lived in houses, but he was insistent and produced a bunch of keys he claimed were for their rooms.

I declined to go with him, however the chicken had enticed me, he then said that if I met him outside Kentucky Chicken that evening, he would buy me some more, he put his finger against his nose and winked saying, he would also have something else I would like, I asked him for details and he simply said it would be a surprise.

The curtains were pulled back and the consultant along with his entourage and my parents were back wanting to speak to my sister, they took one look at the man with white hair and he jumped off the bed and put his arms around two of the females in the group, it was obvious the group knew him.

I went out later that day on the premise of going conker hunting, however I went to the Kentucky Fried Chicken shop, when I arrived, there were a few people waiting for chicken and more eating chicken in the street, then a few minutes later the man arrived, he was no longer wearing the white doctors coat but still had the gold shoes on.

He was greeted by several people and then recognised me, wait here a minute, he said, I will get some chicken and he went into the shop. He returned with a box and led me up a side street to where his car was parked, he opened the back door making some comment about getting inside before it rained, He climbed into the back seat and I climbed in beside him, I was surprised to see a girl I estimated to be fifteen already in the back seat sitting the other side of the man, she was wearing a hospital night gown which I recognised as I had seen my sister in one. The girl did not speak a word, she seemed to know what was going to happen next. He said that she was my surprise he thought I would like, and opened the box of chicken, there were two pieces inside he offered her the first choice, to my dismay, she took the largest piece, he then passed me the box and I took the other.

Whilst eating the chicken, it struck me that it was even nicer when it was hot, I looked over and the man had pulled up the girls' clothing exposing her knickers, he had a hand inside them touching her. Within minutes he turned to me and told me to kneel on the floor of the car, he then took slipped down my trousers as they were two sizes too large for me. He then assaulted me and the girl with one hand each. At the climax, he had bent over and taken my penis into his mouth, he then turned to the girl and kissed her, with my ejaculate still in his mouth.

Suddenly it was all over, and I was out on the pavement watching the car drive away. I could not believe what had just happened, but I knew one thing, I had enjoyed it.

Over the next week or so, every passage from the bible and every church meeting seemed to be themed on the sin of fornication, homosexuality, sex out of wedlock and the story of Sodom and Gomorrah. I felt that God was trying to provide me with the second sex lesson in my life and that everything I had done was irreprehensible.

I was torn, I had really enjoyed my sexual awakening and could not stop thinking about it, finally I determined that I would start to hang around outside the Kentucky Chicken shop and see if I could meet this man again.

After what seemed like weeks, he arrived at the chicken shop, this time very smartly dressed, he saw me and tried to ignore me, talking instead to other people outside the shop. He then went inside, returning with a box, he looked at me and asked if I wanted some more chicken.

I went with him to where he had parked the car and climbed into the back as before, however, the girl was not there, he climbed into the front and drove the car whilst I took my chance to eat the largest of the two pieces of chicken. We arrived and parked next to a building with twin round topped doors and round topped windows either side. I was not sure at the time, but I now believe this building was the chapel in the grounds of St James's Hospital. He said wait here for me and left me in the car.

He returned with the girl I had met in the previous encounter and once again we took up the back seat of his car, she was wearing the same hospital nightgown, but this time had no shoes on, much the same happened only this time he placed my hand on the girl's crotch which increased my arousal and the meeting ended when he once again kissed the girl.

He took the girl from the car and returned later alone. He drove me back heading for the chicken shop, but I asked him to drop me nearer to home. When we stopped, he suddenly turned around and spoke to me saying that I should not try to meet him ever again, and that if he saw me again, I would regret it, he made it very clear that there would not be a third "surprise".

Months passed and I could not forget the encounter and the surprise, however I was regretting my actions, lying to my parents, meeting a stranger, having sex outside marriage, having homosexual sex, and assaulting a young girl who I did not know.

One day, I went with my sister and parents to Leeds General Infirmary to meet the consultant, in the meeting, the consultant wanted my sister to remove her clothes for examination, so I was told to meet up with them again later outside the hospital front door.

Walking down a few corridors I realised I was lost, and I bumped into the man again, he was wearing the white coat again and was pushing a trolley with a patient on it. I asked him to show me the way out of the hospital and he agreed, but only if I helped him to push the trolley first.

We went down some corridors, through several sets of doors and then waited for a lift, when it arrived, we pushed the trolley inside and the doors closed behind us, at that, the man uncovered the woman on the trolley, she was about the same age as my mother I thought, however, I was shocked to see she was dead.

He started to fondle her breasts and kissed her on the mouth, when he stood up, her mouth has open and he closed it with his fingers, looking up at me he gestured that I should do the same, he said something along the lines of "I like them like this, they don't complain". I was shocked into silence and stood as if fixed to the spot, the lift stopped, and he threw the sheet back over the woman and we continued along several more corridors until he told me to wait for him.

I watched as he went through some more doors where he returned a few minutes later without the trolley. We set off to find the exit as he had promised, however just as I could see the doors, he pulled me away and down a few steps of a small staircase, he grabbed hold of me by the left testicle and squeezed so hard I could not make a sound and thought I was going to black out, this is what I will do to you if you tell anyone about this and if I ever see you again, he said.

He let go and walked down the stairs and was gone, I collapsed onto my knees in agony and after several minutes I managed to hobble to the exit and met my sibling and parents. What has happened, said my mother, and I lied to her, I said I had encountered the school bully who had kicked me in the groin.

I was unable to walk so my father put an arm around me and half carried me home. I was unfit for school for a few days and for weeks afterwards, I passed blood and clots and tissue every time I urinated. However, I was too scared to tell anyone what had really happened, as that would mean admitting to breaking numerous rules and would likely get me into serious trouble.

Chapter 3

The consequences of abuse on my life

The encounter with this tall white-haired man lived with me throughout my teenage years, ejaculation was painful and, on several occasions, the pain like toothache, a dull pain which you noticed most at night when trying to sleep. I believed that this was Gods way of punishing me for being so wicked.

My family moved to the other side of the city shortly afterwards, and I thought that this was a good thing as I would not be likely to meet him again. We now had a television set and I now discovered the identity of the tall man; he was on Top of the Pops and Saturday night family show Jim I fix it.

He was Jimmy Savile.

I continued to suffer with the injury to my testicle, but felt I needed to keep this secret, admitting to this injury would raise questions I did not want to answer from my parents, doctor etc. so I suffered in silence. As a result, the injury was never reported.

The new house attic bedrooms were just as cold in winter as the previous house, wearing clothes and even coats to bed was the norm, there were a few hot water bottles but by the time I needed one, they were already in use, it was a simple thing to resolve, have a search around in my sibling's beds until I found one to re fill, usually I would search my brothers beds, however on one particularly cold night my search had come up blank.

I discovered that my sister had masturbated herself to sleep and still had her hand in her knickers, this immediately took me back to Savile's car with his, and later my hand inside the young girl's underwear. I was aroused and retired to my room.

I gave up my religion when I reached sixteen and could drop church and other meetings, this was against my parents' wishes but as an adult, they could no longer demand I attend.

In my teens, I met a girl who became my fiancé and then some years later, my wife. Sex within marriage should have been a pleasurable experience, however I still suffered the toothache type pain afterwards, sometimes for days.

I could not watch Savile on TV, I did bump into him several times in my thirties and forties in the city, he had taken to wearing a disguise comprising a fake nose and large glasses, but it did not provide much cover, he stood out in a crowd due to his hair, height, and choice of clothes. He either did not recognise me or chose to ignore me each time.

I considered tackling him on one occasion when I saw him in a fish and chip restaurant on Street Lane, North Leeds, however he was a professional wrestler, and I was an unfit middle-aged man. He was also one of the most famous celebrities in the UK at the time, so I felt that any complaint I may raise, without absolute proof, would not be considered seriously.

Some years after the injury I became ill, I suffered with horrendous back ache in my lumbar region, over several days this pain moved to my side and then to my injured testicle, then abated. However, it kept coming back and with increased frequency. Eventually I went to my GP, he looked me over and noted my left testicle was twice the size of the other and asked how long it had been like that, I replied, "since I was 12 years old" and he moved on, he diagnosed I was suffering from a trapped nerve and prescribed pain killers, a board in the bed and rest.

The pain, and frequency of recurrence increased over the months and I booked sessions with a chiropractor, he again examined me, noticed the testicle, and asked what my GP had made of it, I gave him the same answers and he moved on. The sessions helped, but the problem got worse.

I was now not hungry, I would leave for work without breakfast, not eat lunch and put off my evening meal until late, after eating I was so bloated, I could not sleep, some weeks passed and I started to lose weight, then I started to vomit up the meal several hours after eating, undigested.

I was no longer fit for work, and was now visiting my GP weekly, no one could explain the symptoms, by this time, my left testicle was hot to touch and very sensitive, I was losing weigh fast and could only keep liquid foods such as soup down, eventually I woke to find I was yellow, jaundice had set in and even the whites of my eyes had changed to yellow, the GP made a visit and diagnosed Hepatitis C she notified the authorities, who arrived to take statements from me with a view to who I had been in contact with.

A few days later, the doctor returned for a check-up, I was still yellow, she told me to report to A&E where I was admitted to hospital as a suspected kidney disease patient. It was close to Christmas and I was in hospital having lost over three stones, passing urine which burned on the way out, so yellow I was unrecognisable when visitors arrived, and if I passed a stool, it was white.

At that point, a lump was detectable in my throat, it was doubling in size every two days and there was obvious concern, I was starved from midnight for a biopsy the following day, which was cancelled. This went on for over a week, starved every night and cancelled every day, eventually I could not speak, the lump was so large. The consultant must have pulled strings because that afternoon I was taken into theatre and a biopsy was taken.

It was Friday, 21 December 1991 when a new consultant arrived to speak to me and my wife, he started to say that I would need to take a course of medication that would make me unfit for work for a period, that may make me feel very ill, but he was confident I would make a recovery, I pushed him on the point and he admitted that he was talking about chemotherapy, that the biopsy had shown I had cancer, that the type of cancer was testicular and that as it had been diagnosed so late, tumours had grown in my abdomen so large that my stomach and other organs could not function, this explained the back ache, the inability to eat, the jaundice, the burning urine and the white stools.

The consultant, Professor Peter Selby, had in 1989 started a dedicated cancer department at St James's hospital in Leeds, to do so his team commandeered every private room in every ward in the hospital for their patients, it was a first in the UK at the time and went on to be so successful that the Bexley wing was opened in 2006, dedicated to cancer care in the north of England, one of the largest and best-equipped cancer centres in Europe this wing even has a hotel on the top floor for visitors and patients to use and is one of the foremost centres for cancer treatment in the world.

Professor Peter Selby advised that he wanted me on his ward the next day by 12:00 and that he personally would oversee the first of four rounds of chemo he thought I would need, each round would comprise a five day stay in hospital followed by two weeks at home recovery time, these hospital periods were known as BEP's.

I asked if I would be able to go home that evening to see my children so close to Christmas and it was agreed that so long as I was back on his ward the next day I could. I arrived home curtesy of a lift from a neighbour and saw my young children, slept in my own bed, and tried to not think too much about how this could be the last time I ever saw my home and family.

The following day, I was assessed for Chemo, and was too ill to start a BEP, instead I received a minute injection, I fell asleep and did not wake for five days.

Whilst I slept, the tumours in my abdomen had shrunk and I started to feel hungry for the first time in many months, a few days later I was sent home with steroids and told to eat and drink to try to recover my fitness that would be needed for me to have the first BEP.

It was six weeks before I was deemed well enough, and I was hospitalised for five days on a drip and given the chemotherapy, I was so weak after this that another BEP could not be started for nine weeks, overall, it took nine months to complete the course and some eight weeks later I had the final surgery to remove that left testicle.

The biopsy showed it was cancer free, but irreparably damaged, I knew how that had happened but did not comment, I was just grateful to be alive.

Whilst it may not be proven that I suffered testicular cancer because of the grievous injury I suffered at the hands of

Savile, it was a coincidence that it occurred in the same testicle, that there was no history of the illness in my family and at the very least, the injury concealed the cancer diagnoses until I was close to death.

Prof Selby, some five years later, in one of the regular clinics I was attended for thirteen years for follow up, let slip that on that Friday when he first met us, he thought the cancer had gone too far and that there was little chance of any recovery, I had been one of his team's early success stories.

As it turns out I was incredibly lucky, Prof Selby had only started the cancer centre in Leeds the previous year, and an anti-hermetic drug, ondansetron, I relied upon during the treatment, had been licenced just weeks before, had I been ill a year earlier, I believe I would not have survived.

My business never recovered fully from my leave of absence of some sixteen months, even when I returned, I was not fully recovered and could not manage the workload, prior to this I had overseen teams of engineers all over the UK commissioning electronic systems, working long hours and staying away.

Just nine years later I was forced to sell the business for a fraction of its true worth, had I been well enough to run it correctly in order to take early retirement, I had another five years of hospital appointments ahead of me, my kidneys and liver were not functioning properly and shortly after I was diagnosed with such high blood pressure that I have to take medication for life, the blood pressure was so high it caused damage to my visual cortex damaging my sight, shortly afterwards I was diagnosed with diabetes and suffered a major heart attack.

There were other consequences, my sister on one of my hot water bottle searches woke up and quizzed what I was doing, I replied I was just looking for a hot water bottle, but I was not sure she believed me. She later told me that she had shared this experience with my younger sister, and that they had both found it very funny at the time.

Some thirty years ago, my youngest sister went for regression therapy to try to understand why her life was so out of control.

Following these sessions, she suddenly claimed that I had sexually abused her every night for three years since she was six. She genuinely believed that this abuse had occurred and spent ten years in tears every night to my parents, whom she had sworn to secrecy, for hours on the phone, Eventually, my parents, after ten years of listening to her, took it upon themselves to write anonymously to the authorities stating that my daughter may be at risk of abuse.

Social services intervened, however after interviewing my daughter, they determined no abuse had occurred.

The letter had been handwritten, and I decided to call and talk to my parents, they admitted to writing the letter following a particularly harrowing phone call from my youngest sister, they believed that no harm would be done, that either abuse was happening, and social services would deal with this, or that no abuse was happening, and no action would be taken. However, what they really achieved was to say that they did not believe I was a fit father to have children. It was necessary to sever all ties with my sister and parents from that day forward.

At the time, I was distraught, and I made the mistake of telling my co directors of the new company I had invested my retirement money and intellectual property into. Three weeks later, my fellow directors changed the names of the signatories on the company bank account, wasted the bank funds on buying stock the company did not need, placed the company into the hands of a receiver and bought the company back by paying off the debt to the bank.

Overnight I lost my income, my investment, my pension pot, and my company. I reported this to the police as in my opinion, changing signatories on the bank account without my signature could not have been accomplished without committing fraud. The police paid scant regard and told me it was a civil matter.

Following the injury to my testicle by Savile, sex had been uncomfortable and sometimes painful, once declared free from cancer, my libido was dramatically reduced following surgery to remove the injured testicle, this and the claims by my little sister, meant I lost interest in sex entirely and have not had sex now for almost 30 years.

Chapter 4

Finally reporting my abuser in 2012

Things changed after Savile died.

On 04 October 2012, ITV broadcast a documentary *the other side of Jimmy Savile,* that alleged he sexually assaulted young girls in his BBC dressing room and in his car. Some five women came forward claiming sexual assault and rape in the 1960's and 1970's.

Suddenly it was clear to me that I (and the girl in the car) were not his only victims, I may be able to tell my story now with a greater chance that I would be believed.

Shortly after, news broke that Savile's headstone was to be removed, 24-hour news channels ran the story every 25 minutes for several days, they showed footage of the gigantic black triple tombstone with gold lettering.

I could see clearly that the stone contained the statement "*It Was Good While It Lasted*". This incensed me, and at the earliest opportunity, I drove to a nearby police station to tell my story.

At that time, unknown to me, the ITV documentary and the 24-hour news coverage spurred hundreds of people to come forward to report abuse spanning several decades. I arrived at the police station on Friday 12 October 2012, at that moment as far as I knew, I was the only male complainant.

Arriving at the police station around 8:00PM, I waited for ages at the front desk to see an officer, I explained briefly that I had been a victim of Savile and wished to make a statement. I was led into an interview room usually used for interrogating criminals, an exceptionally large officer walked into the room with some paper and a pen, he was dressed in full police Friday night drunk riot management uniform, complete with stab vest, high visibility vest, utility belt with handcuffs, etc. mobile phone in a chest pocket, police radio with handset attached above the phone, and high visibility cap. He looked like he had prepared to be working in the city centre Friday night drunk squad but had been redirected to interview me without changing.

Immediately my worst fears were realised, the size of this officer and his attire were intimidating, he his demeanour was more, why are you wasting my time, than sympathetic, he did not have the curtesy to switch off his radio or phone and he was not prepared to record the meeting, hardly using the paper and pen.

I almost did not give an interview. However, he assured me the police were currently dealing with statements from hundreds of victims of Savile, that the case was so large now that the Met police had taken overall control and that I should continue.

I told the officer about meeting Savile in the Leeds General Infirmary; I was able to relate most of the story about the first and second meetings with Savile and about my later hot water bottle searches in my sister's bed.

During the interview, the officer's radio and mobile phone continuously interrupted meaning I had to stop talking and listen to the officer talk on the radio/phone, as a result parts of my story were told out of sequence and parts were forgotten, the effort of finally telling my story to the police was so great that I was pale, shaking and for some parts in tears, however I was offered no comfort whatsoever, noy even a glass of water.

After one longer than average radio interruption making it obvious this officer oversaw a team on active operations at the same time as hearing my witness statement, the officer then started to ask me more details about my seeking out Savile for a second time, he was interested in the girl in the car, he wanted to know details, age, race, clothes, colour of clothes etc. He also wanted to know in detail about my sister, what age was she when this occurred and intimate details.

Suddenly the interview had changed from me volunteering a witness statement, to an interrogation into my having admitted asexually assaulting an underage girl, then seeking out Savile for more, repeating the assault and incestuous acts with my sister.

In the middle of the interrogation, another more senior officer in plain clothes suddenly walked into the room and sat down. He must have been listening to the interview. He wanted to ask more probing questions about the girl, how much had I enjoyed touching her, did I or Savile have penetrative or oral sex with her, did I know how to contact her, why had I wanted to meet her again with Savile, did I know at the time it was wrong and did I know I was committing an offence.

He then started along a different line, victims of sexual abuse, he claimed, are normally ashamed and hurt by their abusers, they do not enjoy the abuse and do not seek out more etc.

He also wanted much greater detail about my sister, ages, dates, times, did I touch her and much more.

I was no longer listening fully, I started to feel that I was the monster here rather than the victim, the girl would not have suffered another assault, had I not sought out Savile for a second encounter, and I wished I had never mentioned my sister, this was distracting the police and they were now interviewing me as the abuser.

I had dug myself into a hole now, so I stopped digging and clammed up. I chose not to talk about the third encounter with Savile and the dead woman, or the physical injury I had suffered at his hand.

The plain clothes officer prodded and pushed for more detail, his voice was raised in frustration and anger at the lack of detail I was providing, despite the occurrences happening over forty years earlier. He was saying things like "are you sure you have told us everything" and "failure to include any details could be deemed as obstructing our enquiry" and "you should tell us the full story to ensure we can treat your statement correctly and ascertain any criminality disclosed" and "you are aware that incest is a crime".

During all the above questioning, the first officers' radio and phone continued to interrupt, however the plain clothed officer just kept talking through the distracting interruptions.

The plain clothed officer then took over and the large officer in full Friday night drunk squad riot gear left the room. I noticed that he had only written about twenty words on the pad he was using to record the interview now in its third hour, my name, address, phone number and email address along with the word's "girl", "sister" and "underage" which were circled. The remaining officer now calmed down and started to discuss what would happen next.

The case had been taken over by the Met police who he said would contact me in due course to take a formal statement and consider what I had said, I was now convinced I was to be arrested for the two assaults I had admitted to with the fifteen-year-old girl and for the admission of looking at my sister.

The interview terminated and the officer unlocked the door to the front desk area, the officer reminded me to expect to hear from the Met police and I left.

I was now in a state of considerable concern and fear, my family were totally unaware I had been a victim, yet the Met police were likely now to call at my home for more information or arrive unannounced to arrest me.

I think readers will agree, this was not the way to conduct an interview with a vulnerable abuse victim volunteering to give a statement after over forty years.

I was not offered a drink, a comfortable environment in which to make a statement, counselling or even comfort and was left traumatised having provided an incomplete statement despite the threats made to force me to tell everything.

That evening I could not sleep, so I used the time to write down everything I could recollect telling the police in the interview, simply to create a record of the meeting, which as far as I could tell, the west Yorkshire police had not done.

It Was Good While It Lasted

Chapter 5

Taking stock & managing the fallout

The television news channels were reporting that hundreds of people had come forward to provide statements, the tombstone was removed from Savile's grave to prevent reprisals/vandalism. The women featuring in the ITV interview were appearing on more programs along with more female victims.

The news channels carried an interview with a solicitor, Liz Dux, she was advising victims to come forward and contact her for victim support, representation and to benefit from her knowledge of historical abuse cases. I called her on Monday and discussed my situation, I was offered a no win no fee contract which I accepted.

Liz requested a copy of my notes from the police interview and I emailed these to her, I notified her that my family were unaware I had been a victim and at here suggestion I created an email address for all communication going forward. Liz advised the Met police that they should only communicate via the email address and I started to feel a bit better, my only concern now was if I were arrested by the Met.

I sat down and wrote out the full statement in detail as far as I could recollect, this time including the incident with the dead woman and the injury. I emailed this to Liz.

Liz wrote a week later advising that I must place a claim with CICA before Friday, as on that date they would be reducing any pay-outs for victims of criminal injuries and I may lose out, I contacted them and filed a claim, this was not easy as the forms provided simply did not fit with historical and multiple incident claims.

A week later CICA, despite my writing on the form my contact email address and the requirement for confidentiality, called my home telephone number. Fortunately, I answered the call and was on my own so could speak, they insisted on sending copies of my claim form by post to my home for signature and would not accept any other communication route. For the next five days, I had to ensure I got to the post first to receive the documents as my wife usually opens mail addressed to either of us.

Out of the blue in January, the Met police called my home number, spoke to one of my children and stated that he was an officer from the Met, he was part of operation Yewtree and that he wanted to speak to me. I was passed the phone and had to walk off into another room to talk, my son had told my wife about the call by the time I returned, and both required an explanation of why the Met Operation Yewtree wanted to speak to me, which was not easy.

The officer advised that they may not require my statement, as in his words they already had enough witnesses. He went on to say that there were hundreds of victims coming forward and that if they needed to contact me, they would in future use the email address I had provided.

I emailed Liz Dux who was disappointed in the actions of the Met, so she sent them a copy of my written statement to ensure the crimes I had reported were included in their investigation.

The next month, Liz emailed to request a meeting with one of her team to capture a full statement from me about the abuse, she asked me to nominate somewhere we could meet for this and I was a bit flummoxed as I did not know how I could do this, in the end we met in a quiet pub and went over my statement for about 2 hours to obtain an official version, including details of my childhood and the consequences of the abuse on my life.

Next it was the turn of the West Yorkshire Police, they telephoned my home number, again ignoring my request for all communication by email. We agreed to meet at a local police station and I duly arrived on the day, I was concerned about the last interview held at the same station, I was concerned I may be arrested and charged, I was expecting Liz Dux or one of her team to attend the interview as I had notified her of the location, time and date of the meeting and I was concerned that no solicitor arrived.

It turned out that the officer I was meeting had written out a statement, he had read my supplied statement via Liz Dux and had re written the salient points that interested the police in the language used by the police for statements, the police were not concerned at my childhood upbringing, or at the consequences and effect the abuse had on my life, they stated that as a minor I had not committed any crime in touching the girl in Savile's car and that the subsequent hot water bottle searches with my sister. They were only interested in the meeting with Savile in which I was groomed, the two incidents in his car and the final meeting with the dead woman and punishment injury caused.

I was asked to read and sign each page of the handwritten statement, which I did. I was then advised that the police, uniquely in history, had decided to record the allegations of the victims as crimes committed by the deceased, Savile, posthumously. I was advised that 208 crimes had been recorded in this way, and four of these were based on my statement. Two counts of sexual abuse of a minor, one count of gross indecency and one count of actual bodily harm.

Liz Dux, upon receiving my complaint that she had not been present simply said that she would not have been permitted to attend the signing of a witness statement, she had not considered how I felt, returning to be interviewed at the same police station where I had been treated as complicit in sexual abuse of a minor and incest.

Chapter 6

Invitation to meet the Speaking Out inquiry

A few weeks later, I happened to intercept the postman in my garden and one of the items of post addressed to me was an invitation from the inquiry team responsible for looking into the Savile scandal within the NHS/DOH.

It transpired that Liz Dux company had passed contact details from all their clients affected by the Savile scandal to the inquiry team. Once again, no care to accept my wishes to protect my family from discovering my victim status had been taken.

I emailed Liz Dux and she wrote to the NHS/DOH to affirm the requirement for communicating with me by email.

Shortly afterwards I received emails from Liz Dux and the NHS/DOH inquiry team, I was being requested to attend a meeting at the Leeds General Infirmary entitled "Speaking Out". I was assured that they wished to meet with as many victims as possible and listen to their stories, this would assist the inquiry in making recommendations for the NHS/DOH and would ensure that no such scandal could ever reoccur. On this basis, I agreed to meet them to ensure they understood my story.

I felt it was my duty to attend and talk to the Speaking Out team, if nothing else, perhaps my story contained unique information that would help the inquiry, I agreed to a date for the meeting and supplied this back to Liz Dux so she or one of her representatives could be present.

The date for the meeting arrived and I found a parking spot immediately meaning I was forty minutes early. I was introduced to the inquiry team, Ray Galloway, and Claire Jones, I was invited to join them in an interview room and given a hot drink. I stated that I was expecting either Liz Dux or a representative from her firm to join me for the meeting. However, no one had arrived yet.

We started to talk, initially friendly and Ray Galloway stated that the inquiry team had received a copy of my statement as made to Liz Dux company and asked if I wanted to add anything further or simply submit the written statement. With the understanding that I was there to be listened to, I advised I would like to speak.

I started to tell the story of my childhood religious upbringing, poor due to my mother resigning her professional career and that we had no radio, TV, or car. I believed this has a bearing on the way I was groomed by and ultimately abused by Savile. I intended to detail the consequences on my life and career after the abuse. I though the team would wish to hear more about me than just what had been included in the written statement. However, the team were not interested in listening to me speak.

Cutting me short, the team started to ask questions about details in my written statement, they refused to accept that as I had been brought up in a family with no radio or TV, that I and my sister had not recognised Savile as he was so famous. They refused to accept that as a boy, despite being raised in a family without a car, I would not know the make of the car used by Savile when he assaulted me and the girl, only that it was large as in their opinion, boys always new about cars.

They called into question the likelihood that Savile, one of the most famous people in the UK, would risk assaulting two young children in daylight in his car whilst parked in a public place.

They refused to accept that the location given for the second incident in Savile's car was in fact on the premises of St James's Hospital, I was forced to state that it was my best recollection of the location, this was not satisfactory.

They then laid out the procedures used by all hospitals in dealing with a deceased person. Clare detailed the procedures step by step, then Ray, starting with the words, can you see there is a problem here, called into question my account, he stated that I could not have witnessed what I claimed, Savile in a lift with a trolley upon which had the body of a woman, because the procedures in pace in hospitals would have prevented this.

They stated that as I had admitted to looking at one of my sisters in my written statement, and that my younger sister had many years later made accusations of abuse, also in my statement, why should they believe that I had not indeed abused both sisters. I managed to splutter out a response that she had only been six at the time and it was the sight of pubic hair, hands, knickers etc which had caused me to become aroused. They sat back for a minute and looked at each other. Then came the attack, Ray Galloway said, you did not say that you knew it would be wrong.

Approximately forty minutes had elapsed, no solicitor had arrived, and I was in a state of shock and confusion, I was now in no doubt that I had been mis led into attending the inquiry, and that the main purpose of this meeting was not to listen to victims to learn from them, but to question their accounts with a view to determining civil liability.

At this point, Ray announced that the interview was now to start formerly and that he would be recording it. He switched on a recorder and both he and Claire announced their names, the purpose of the interview etc. I was in no fit state to be interviewed and had no one with me for support, but the interview kicked off regardless.

During the recorded interview both Claire and Ray repeated parts of what had already been said for the recording, it was described as highly unlikely that I had been assaulted in a car in public along with an underage girl by someone as famous and recognisable as Savile. It was described as highly unlikely that I had been assaulted in a car in the grounds of a hospital along with an underage girl for the same reason. It was described as impossible that I had witnessed Savile, pushing a trolley by himself with a dead woman upon it, again it was stated that hospitals had procedures in place, that these procedures prevented any one person from processing and transporting a deceased person, and would absolutely prevent the transporting of a deceased person covered only with a sheet. It was described as highly unlikely that someone as recognisable as Savile had assaulted me as I had described so close to the public entrance of a major hospital.

At that point, I started to lose my temper and asked silly questions about how long hospitals had had such procedures about deceased persons, could Savile have collected the body from A&E or even off an ambulance. I was rebuffed on all questions and told that the procedures were the same in the 1970's, and that they applied in both A&E and when someone died in an ambulance.

I tried to say that other victims had told stories like mine about Savile abusing them in his car, and that footage of

Savile abusing a young girl on Top of The Pops during a live show had been found and broadcast on the news. This really piqued their interest and they started to ask how much I had read/watched about Savile in the news and on TV.

The conclusions they drew were that I had concocted a story based upon news and TV documentaries. I was now flustered and out of control, I believed incorrectly they had my statement given to Liz Dux *and* a copy of my police statement I had authorised they obtain; however, they only had the former. Knowing the content of both, I blurted out about how I had been interviewed by the police, and reasons why my police statement was different to my full statement, because the police did not want to record some elements included in my full account.

The interview closed and the recording was switched off, however they had not finished yet, they went on to discuss more details from my written statement and what were the differences between this and my police statement, I tried to explain how I had been interviewed, and how I had not felt I could tell the whole story due to the way the interview was held etc.

Ray Galloway just stated he was concerned that my police interview and my recorded statement were different despite my protestations that the sections detailing my encounters with Savile were the same, only the preamble and consequences of the abuse sections had been dropped from the police statement.

That concluded the visit, I was physically shaking and obviously upset by the way in which the meeting had been conducted, when Claire Jones asked me if I would like to be referred for the psychiatric care package, they were offering all witnesses who came forward, I replied that I would like that and I left the room.

Chapter 7

Speaking Out – was not about listening to victims!

Immediately after arriving home I emailed Liz Dux, I was fuming, once again she had not attended to support me, I felt I had been tricked into attending an adversarial interview during which I had been primed to fail before the recorded section started, that my story had been called into doubt and I had not been believed, and once again, not listened to.

I received a curt, unsympathetic reply from Liz, she claimed that she would not have been able to provide support during my meeting with the speaking out inquiry even had she attended, that the inquiry team had the right to question my statement and test the evidence as would a court of law, that had she attended it would have only been in the capacity of a witness, with no powers to advise or intervene.

I was fuming that I had been conned into attending the meeting, I now wished I had never come forward.

Later she apologised for seeming harsh in her letter, she then asked me if there was anything, I could provide by way of evidence that supported my claims, witnesses, times, and dates etc.

I replied that I may be able to get my sister to provide a statement and advised that the NHS/DOH may wish to look at her medical records for times and dates when she had been admitted to hospital, however my sister was dying from a degenerative disease and whilst she said, when asked, that she could recall the meeting in hospital with Savile and the chicken, she was not fit to be interviewed and has subsequently died.

A few months later I received more information from Liz Dux, a compensation package for victims was to be set up using the funds remaining in Savile's estate for victims not connected with the NHS or the BBC, who would be awarded compensation by one or the other of these organisations.

Eventually months later and following appeals by Savile's estate a scale of tariffs was made available, the letter was provided only to the victims who were all advised it must not be disclosed. The lowest tariff was for sexual assault over clothes, £1500, rising to rape. An uplift of 50% would be applied to victims who had suffered more than once.

In my case, it stated that the appropriate tariff would be for sexual assault under clothes, £9250 including an uplift, because it had occurred more than once. There was no agreed tariff for trauma from witnessing sexual assault of a dead woman, and no tariff agreed for physical assault. At that moment I knew that I had not been believed and that my claim would ultimately be rejected.

A year after the meeting with the inquiry team, I received emails from Claire Jones and Ray Galloway and the NHS/DOH solicitors' team on the same day via Liz Dux, the Speaking Out team wanted more information from me as they were finalising their reports, the DOH legal team wanted the same, but to ensure I was not about to pull a cat out of the bag after they rejected my claim.

They were asking if I had tracked down the girl I had met in Savile's car and if so, would she be providing a statement in support of my claim.

They asked if I had obtained my sister's medical records to prove she had been in hospital when I claimed we met Savile.

They asked if I could provide dates and times for the meetings with Savile.

They also asked for medical records for myself covering the period immediately after Savile crushed my testicle.

Quite how they thought I would be able to recall such details over forty years after the events when I was around twelve years old at the time, I am unsure.

In addition, how could I obtain my sister's medical records, these are confidential. However, I was sure that the NHS/DOH had the means to obtain them.

How could they expect records, when I had stated in my witness testimony and in the inquiry Speaking Out meeting that I had not disclosed the injury to avoid difficult questions I dd not wish to answer.

It Was Good While It Lasted

Chapter 8

Victim status denied

My wife started to complain that living with me was like living with a bear with a sore head, I would snap at her and my family without reason and spent hours awake at night mulling over the circumstances of the abuse and its consequences, I found myself typing notes to try to assist me with sleeping. I decided I had waited long enough for the psychiatric care I had been offered.

I wrote to Liz Dux again to advise her that I had not heard from Claire with an appointment for the psychiatric care package she had offered. I reminded Liz she had written to them to remind them of this, some five months after the meeting, with no reply.

Liz replied that she had obtained a response from the Speaking Out team, they had stated that if I required psychiatric care, I should go to my GP. Caring as always.

I wrote in confidence to my GP giving the bare bones of the story and asking for help. He met with me after surgery hours one evening and I told him the whole story.

He arranged for a fact-finding meeting with the psychiatric care team in my area.

A few weeks later I attended a meeting, and it was determined I would benefit most from psychoanalytic psychiatric care, a service not normally available on the NHS. However, my GP pushed for this and I duly receive my first meeting almost three years after the speaking out meeting.

Shortly after this I received a curt letter from Liz Dux simply stating that my claim had been rejected by the NHS/DOH and that there was nothing further they could do for me. That they were dropping me as a client with immediate effect. The letter advised that if I disagreed with the outcome, I should take the DOH to court. However, this would be expensive, public and in their opinion would likely fail.

I was understandably annoyed, I recalled when the inquiry was published, Kate Lampard was visibly distressed at the findings which detailed numerous occasions when Savile had abused dead bodies, and that he had been granted unconditional access to two morgues, one of which was in the Leeds General Infirmary.

In addition, Jeremy Hunt the health secretary had stood in the house of commons and said that for too long the victims of Savile had not been believed, and "the victims must be believed".

I collated my notes written at night along with sections of my statement and other documents and wrote a twelve-page letter to the Health Secretary, Jeremy Hunt MP.

My letter detailed the encounters with Savile, the reasons I had not come forward for over forty years, the way in which I had been treated by the police, solicitors, speaking out inquiry team, DOH solicitors, the breaches of confidentiality and the lack of professional care.

I advised him that I had not been believed by the Speaking Out inquiry team despite my claims of assault in Savile's car being supported by other witness testimony included in the inquiry report.

That the final inquiry had detailed twelve incidents in which Savile had been witnessed acting inappropriately with patients who had died, not following hospital procedures.

That at the time I wrote my full account for Liz Dux and the Met police, October 2012, the fact that Savile had unrestricted access to the morgue at Leeds General Infirmary and had abused his position as volunteer porter to handle cadavers, was not in the public domain, hence this part of my statement could not have been invented.

I reminded him of his speech in the house and asked him to personally investigate the handling of my case by the inquiry team.

I also wrote to Liz Dux, I berated her for the way my case had been handled and her lack of care.

I requested copies of all documents she held on file in my name.

Her reply was astonishing, she defended her actions despite these being indefensible, she even tried to say that the outcome of the speaking Out meeting was entirely my fault, and that I had not needed to attend the meeting in the first place.

However, she did supply me with around eight documents from her file, my statement to her colleague, my redacted statement to the police, her letter to Claire Jones asking her to chase up my psychiatric support, my original notes from the police interview and subsequent statement, a letter from the DOH solicitors requesting my sister's medical records etc.

Also, the letter from the DOH legal department rejecting my claim, signed by the Health Minister, Jeremy Hunt MP.

I now realised I had wasted my time writing to Jeremy Hunt, and took a multiple route strategy to hopefully get someone to listen and possibly correct the injustice of the DOH legal team's decision. To deny my victim status without having met me.

I filed a complaint with the DOH citing that my statement described assaults which fit exactly Savile's MO. That the inquiry team statement, that I could not have witnessed Savile with a dead body due to procedures in place in hospitals, was risible as it relied upon Savile following the hospital's procedures, which he clearly did not, and that the fact Savile had access to the morgue and cadavers were not in the public domain at the time of my statement.

I received a reply from the DOH in under a week, it advised me that there was no right of appeal against the decision taken, that the only way I could challenge the decision would be to take the DOH to court, and warned me that this would be public, costly and there would be no guarantee of success hence I should seek legal advice.

I also wrote to the DOH solicitors requesting an interview, in which I wished them to explain why my case had been rejected without meeting with me. They wrote back to say that they would not be prepared to meet me.

Chapter 9

Getting my MP involved

I wrote to my MP Fabian Hamilton.

He contacted me shortly afterwards to ask for copies of documents I held, which I duly emailed to him, a few days later he wanted to meet me, so I went to his surgery late one evening to meet him privately.

His secretary was present for the meeting to take minutes and I told my story from the beginning, after around ninety minutes, it was obvious that Fabian was visibly upset on hearing my story, angry my victim status had been denied, incredulous at the statement that I could not have witnessed what I claim (Savile with the dead woman) because procedures were in place to prevent such an occurrence, and determined to help me as much as possible.

It was my opinion that Fabian and his secretary had never heard a story like mine before and would never forget what they had heard.

Fabian Hamilton waited a few weeks for Jeremy Hunt to make a further statement about Savile in the house, and asked questions on my behalf, this can be seen recorded in Hansard.

Fabian received a letter from Jeremy Hunt shortly afterwards, it was non-committal, dismissive and did not offer much hope, however it contained two things which were in my favour, it stated that he had read my letter, further, it had a handwritten codicil, a few words of hope by the signature, asking for a meeting with Fabian.

Shortly after my MP met the Health Minister, it was agreed that Kate Lampard would be asked to investigate the circumstances of how the meeting between myself and the Speaking Out inquiry team had been conducted.

She wanted details from me giving her direction and the scope of my complaint, I wrote to her directly detailing how the meeting had been held for forty minutes without notes or recordings, prior to tearing me apart in the recorded formal session that followed.

I detailed to her that the inquiry had published its intentions and scope prior to holding interviews, these included the fact that the inquiry did not have the scope to determine civil or criminal liability, yet the meeting I attended had been used to determine the DOH civil liability in my case.

I advised her that the same document detailed that all meetings with victims and witnesses would be digitally recorded, transcribed and copies supplied to said witnesses/victims for checking prior to anonymous inclusion in the final report, this clearly did not happen with my meeting as forty minutes were not recorded or transcribed.

I went on to say why I felt my encounters with Savile had met Savile's MO and that this was borne out in the witness testimonies provided to the multiple inquiries into his abuse and cited witness statements from DOH and BBC inquiries describing sexual abuse of minors, in his car, in public.

Finally, I once again advised her of my primary complaint, my case was rejected on the grounds I could not have witnessed what I claim because procedures were in place in hospitals which prevented this. I read the sections of the inquiries into Leeds teaching hospitals and Stoke

Mandeville hospital detailing Savile's behaviour with cadavers and morgues, both had permitted Savile inappropriate access. I copied no less than twelve witness testimonies from these two published inquiries. Some were compelling and showed that Savile did not follow hospital procedures around the handling of the dead.

One was a story from Stoke Mandeville in which a mortuary attendant raised a formal recorded complaint against Savile for transporting the body of a young boy to the morgue in a pram.

Another was an eyewitness account of a ward sister on night shift who, returning from a break, witnessed Savile pushing a deceased patient by himself off the ward, she asked him "where are you going with that" only to be told by Savile without stopping "the morgue", she then stated that she called after him asking how will you get in it's closed, and Savile just waved a bunch of keys then continued out of the ward.

Only about a week later, Kate Lampard met with Jeremy Hunt and Fabian Hamilton to advise them that she was sure that the meeting between myself and the Speaking Out team had been held correctly and that she upheld the conclusions they had reached.

It seemed I had reached the end of the road with my complaint, I was not fortunate enough to have funds to take on the NHS/DOH in court, and as I wished to remain anonymous such action would be public and therefore precluded. Further, I did not wish to contact the press, as typically my story would become their story and twisted/redacted/changed to suit their agenda.

It Was Good While It Lasted

Chapter 10

The Parliamentary Ombudsman

I reviewed the DOH complaints procedure one last time looking for anything that would permit me to continue the complaint. I discovered that once my MP had been involved, I could ask him to support a complaint to the Parliamentary and Health Service Ombudsman. Their website starts with the words "We make final decisions on complaints that have not been resolved by the NHS in England and UK government departments and other public organisations." And "We do this fairly and without taking sides. Our service is free."

At last, this appeared to be a path I could take, anonymously and without great financial risk. I wrote to Fabian Hamilton and he immediately agreed to support my complaint with the ombudsman.

Initially the Ombudsman requested copies of documents I had sent to my MP Fabian Hamilton, so I emailed everything I had including the letters to Jeremy Hunt MP and Kate Lampard.

I received a reply advising that in their opinion I had a valid case for the DOH to answer, but they required more documents, so I emailed everything I had, including my statement to the police, the police notification that four crimes had been recorded due to my testimony, my statement to Liz Dux, my copy of the interview with the Speaking Out inquiry and emails between myself and Liz Dux in-between.

Months elapsed, but I finally received notice that the Ombudsman had accepted my complaint and would now be requesting documents from the DOH legal team.

I was provided with a document detailing the areas the Ombudsman could investigate in their capacity, this was surprisingly short, however it did include an agreement to investigate the way my claim had been processed.

Surprisingly, the ombudsman advised that unlike the financial ombudsman, should they find evidence that supported my claim, they did not have the power to insist that the DOH put me back into the financial position I would have been, had they accepted my claim. At best any compensation would be awarded to reflect the mistakes they may uncover.

A year passed, during which the Ombudsman changed to a new person Rob Behrens CBE, the member of the team dealing with my complaint left and I was back too square one. It was suggested that a meeting would be beneficial, and I booked a small hotel meeting room in Leeds for the date agreed.

A close friend and confidant had become involved at this point, he knew what had happened and had been given access to the documents and I had discussed all aspects of the case with him, we both attended the meeting, and when my case handler arrived, she was with her boss, a male employee within the ombudsman service. Our first thoughts were that he was supporting my case handler to tell me that my complaint would not be upheld.

However, the two representatives from the ombudsman sat and listened to my story for over two hours, you could tell they had never had a complaint of this nature before, and that neither would ever forget the meeting. They asked a lot of questions, and for once, they took copious notes.

They went on to say that the delay was from the DOH who had not yet provided the documents they required to investigate my case, they stated that the DOH legal team were claiming client confidentiality as the reason not to supply the documents and were refusing to accept that they were legally obliged to assist the Ombudsman.

The DOH legal team took the view that they could reject the Ombudsman's requests on the grounds that they considered the witness accounts of Savile's behaviour as just that, witness accounts, not crimes. Despite the police recording these as crimes committed by Savile posthumously, as such, because they claimed that these were not crimes, they did not have the same level of responsibility to the Ombudsman to cooperate, what an arrogant standpoint.

When quizzed on this point, and why they had allowed a year to elapse waiting for the DOH legal team to comply with their request, they were visibly embarrassed, stated that my former case handler, who had now left, was not senior enough to handle my case and that they, the serious cases team, had now taken over my complaint and guaranteed rapid progress going forward.

Pushed harder, they went on to say that their chief executive Amanda Campbell had taken a personal interest in the case and it was her who would be filing a new demand for the documents held by the DOH legal team.

At the end of the meeting, we parted without being any further ahead, the ombudsman's case handlers now needed to discuss the case to determine what, if anything, they could do. The final departing agreement was that they would keep me up to date with my claims progress.

I received an updated document from the Ombudsman containing a record of the meeting, which was accurate and agreed the new scope of my complaint.

They could and intended to discover how the DOH legal team had determined that my claim was to be denied. It confirmed that the Ombudsman, having the same powers of a high court judge, could demand the DOH legal team comply and release their documents, thereby overruling the claim of client confidentiality.

At last, I was starting to get somewhere, it now looked positive that my complaint would be scrutinised in full and that I may at some point understand why my claim had been denied.

I was still suffering from inability to sleep, I was constantly mulling over the whole ghastly story in my mind, writing down anything I could recollect to form around a hundred pages of notes. I would wake at all hours and run the whole story through my mind, re-enacting the stages as I recalled them, looking for where I went wrong, considering how I might one day resolve matters with my sister and my parents, wondering if my sister really did believe her stories, she had discussed about me which were, in my opinion, an obvious cry for help. Wondering if I should pursue my fellow directors for the fraud they committed, and the bank who permitted the signature to be changed, then took security for the loan claiming the intellectual property, patents, and registered designs, to secure a loan which was already secured by the Government.

My wife was delighted when the first appointment for psychiatric care arrived.

Months passed without any updates so I wrote to the Ombudsman and received a few non-committal words email reply, it said that things were complicated and there was no update they could provide at this time.

More months elapsed with no update, so I wrote to Amanda Campbell, the chief executive and deputy Ombudsman with a list of facts, she replied in a much longer email advising that the DOH were still refusing to cooperate with the Ombudsman, that the certainty of the Ombudsman's powers to demand the release of the documents and cooperation was now receding as more complex arguments had been developed by the DOH legal team, she did however state that she had a meeting booked with the DOH legal team to discuss my case in a few weeks' time and hoped to progress my complaint soon.

She then went on to advise that the DOH legal team would be happy to have a meeting with me to discuss my case, despite refusing to meet me some years before at my request.

I declined to have a face-to-face meeting with them as I could not see how this could help, when they were refusing to cooperate with the Ombudsman.

It Was Good While It Lasted

Chapter 11

Ray Galloway, the Speaking Out team

I discovered that Ray Galloway who interviewed me in the Speaking Out inquiry is a former detective superintendent with North Yorkshire Police and may have had links to Savile.

A news article published in Whitby News states; -

One of the members of the investigation team is Detective Superintendent Ray Galloway (retired), formerly the Director of North Yorkshire Police Force Intelligence, who commanded its Force Intelligence Bureau I believe until his retirement in January 2013. He is internationally famous for his investigation of the disappearance of Claudia Lawrence

This is of interest because in July 2007 North Yorkshire Police received an enquiry from Surrey Police for any intelligence they had on Jimmy Savile. The Bureau sent back a negative response. However, in fact Savile was well known as an associate of the known paedophile Peter Jaconelli. Detectives from North Yorkshire Police had apparently questioned witnesses about Savile in the 2003 investigation referred to above.

The Surrey Police investigation was the best chance that existed of bringing Savile to justice. It failed because:

A police officer referred to as "Inspector 5" of West Yorkshire Police who was a member of Savile's notorious "Friday Morning Tea Club" (a regular gathering for twenty years, of senior officers for tea with Savile while they were on duty, where Savile alleged "blackmail letters" i.e. complaints about Savile were destroyed) rang Surrey Police and arranged for Savile to be interviewed at Stoke Mandeville Hospital instead of being interviewed at a police station.

North Yorkshire Police Force Intelligence Bureau failed to pass on the intelligence they undoubtedly had about Savile and Jaconelli, to the Surrey investigation. It should be further noted that the Force Intelligence Bureau features prominently in the series of articles on corruption and misconduct in North Yorkshire Police called Operation Countryman II which we will be running shortly.

I found it intriguing that an officer who had access to all force intelligence and therefore may have had knowledge of the original bungled investigation into Savile and Jaconelli was also involved in the present NHS investigation. I therefore asked the following additional questions of Mr Galloway.

- At what date did Mr Galloway take up his appointment as Director of Force Intelligence?
- Did he know or meet Jimmy Savile at any time either socially or through his duties?
- Was he a member of Savile's Friday Morning Tea Club?
- Does he know if any officers of North Yorkshire Police were members of the Friday Morning Tea Club?
- Did he at any time know Inspector Mick Starkey or any other member of the Friday Morning Tea Club?
- Did he know or meet Peter Jaconelli, (NAME REDACTED) or Jimmy Corrigan at any time either socially or through his duties?
- Was he involved at all in the investigation into Rutter and White in 2003?

- Does he have any explanation for the failure of North Yorkshire Police to pass on information to the Surrey investigation?

I received the following prompt and courteous response from a Leeds Teaching Hospitals spokesman:

"I have put this question to Mr Galloway and he has confirmed he was not the Director of Intelligence for North Yorkshire Police in July 2007, nor has he ever been involved, in any way whatsoever, with any investigation or enquiry relating to Jimmy Savile. He does not wish to add any more to that statement. Reporting to the formal panel is an investigation team, their names and roles are spelled out on a separate public website set up specifically for the investigation, which is accessible via the link below:

http://www.speakingoutleeds.co.uk/

when you go on to that site click on investigation in the menu in the top left and then scroll down to the membership.

As you will see it includes brief biographies for the investigation team members, including Mr Galloway. This sets outs the why Mr Galloway is suitably qualified to be involved in the Leeds investigation, and you will also note that there are a number of other well qualified and independent individuals who are part of the same team.

I really don't have anything else I can add on the matters you raised relating to Mr Galloway or North Yorkshire Police – as I said in my last message these are not questions for our Trust."

Clearly, having a retired senior police officer on the team is an asset to the investigation. Having taken up an appointment to an investigation of this nature of his own free will, Mr Galloway has accepted a duty to behave openly and has voluntarily agreed to some degree of public scrutiny of his experience and credentials.

Given the public allegations that blatant corruption in North Yorkshire Police allowed Jaconelli and Savile to operate openly in Scarborough, because of Jaconelli's position as Mayor and his close connections to the Police and the Council; that there is now potentially a link between Savile's offending at the LGI (in the West Yorkshire Police Area, where one police officer has been referred to the IPCC) and Jaconelli and Savile's offending in Scarborough (in the North Yorkshire Police area), it seems to me to be completely unsatisfactory that Mr Galloway refuses to answer these questions and carries on as a member of the investigation with this unresolved conflict of interest.

Under these circumstances, it appears to me that the integrity of the Leeds Teaching Hospitals NHS Trust investigation is fatally compromised.

A spokesperson for the trust responded to this concern:

"We do not intend to answer the questions you raise whilst the investigation is underway. We do not accept that the investigation into Jimmy Savile's activities is in any way compromised or flawed and are assured that it is being conducted with the utmost integrity."

I can only pose the question: If indeed this is the case, why should Mr Galloway refuse to answer the above questions about any knowledge he or North Yorkshire Police may or may not have had about Savile's close associate and fellow paedophile Jaconelli? Particularly as a simple answer confirming he knew nothing would resolve these concerns and add to the credibility of the investigation.

Full article published here http://www.real-whitby.co.uk/jimmy-savile-the-hospitals-investigation/

This report puts Ray Galloway under suspicion and therefore unfit to be part of the inquiry team. ,If as stated by the Speaking Out inquiry to my solicitor Liz Dux, the interview process was not intended to be confrontational. Why select Ray Galloway to conduct the interviews, when his general demeanour is confrontational.

I passed this information to the Ombudsman for consideration.

Mr Galloway was unfit to interview witnesses/victims.

More recently, The BBC have called into question Det Supt Ray Galloway's handling of the Claudia Lawrence unsolved murder case. The testimony provided shows just what sort of character Ray Galloway was. It says, -

Joan (Claudia's mother) has long been critical of the first police investigation. She says officers initially used a photo of Claudia with the wrong hair colour and that she wasn't spoken to in the immediate aftermath of her daughter's disappearance.

Ray Galloway came to see me once, a few days [later]. He never asked me what Claudia was like, what her hobbies were, he didn't want to get to know her.

I told [police] that she didn't look like that when she disappeared - her hair was much darker, but they carried on using that [photo] for a number of years.

By June, the case had taken a different direction. Its lead detective told BBC Crimewatch that investigators were now focusing on allegations made about the chef's love life.

"Who was Claudia going out with? Who was she seeing?" Mr Galloway asked viewers. "Who was her boyfriend? Who was showing her maybe some unhealthy interest?"

In a second appearance on the show he made more direct claims, describing Claudia's relationships as "complex and mysterious" - words that immediately became the subject of tabloid headlines.

"It set the rumour mill whirring," says former Met detective chief inspector Clive Driscoll. He believes Mr Galloway's comments turned public opinion against her and had a detrimental effect on the investigation.

"The way Ray Galloway went about it was wrong, he should have phrased it differently," he says.

"It painted a picture that Claudia somehow deserved what happened to her. It had a big impact on how people viewed her and subsequently how the public responded to the investigation."

Mr Galloway, who is no longer with the force, was contacted by the BBC about points raised in this article. He declined to comment.

Mr Galloway's public comments about Claudia's "secret relationships" were indeed seized upon by journalists.

"Claudia's sex life, her alleged affairs, were represented in the press as being of key relevance to her case and status as a victim," says Dr Charlotte Barlow, criminology lecturer at Lancaster University.

"Some of the main phrases used to refer to her were things like 'scarlet woman' or 'home-wrecker' and it's this kind of narrative and language which has underlying, highly gendered assumptions."

Dr Barlow says such wording is only really used to describe female victims and represents them as somehow responsible for their fate.

"However, the blame and focus here should always be on the perpetrator, ensuring that they are held to account, and never on the victim."

Dr Karen Shalev-Greene, director for the Centre for the Study of Missing Persons, says there is often an element of "victim hierarchy" in how the press portray missing people.

"The most 'innocent' victims get an almost angelic coverage while those with more 'complex' lives are portrayed differently, without a thought to the victim or the family."

Police suspected that Claudia had several lovers over a number of years - not unusual for a single woman of her age who was actively dating.

But when coupled with the suggestion that some of them were married, she was seen as "the other woman".

The picture painted of Claudia in the press was not one her friends recognised. "If this was a man, this kind of behaviour would not have been an issue," says Suzy.

"There was a marked change when the salacious stories started," adds Jen.

"They didn't mention Claudia the great friend, the loving daughter, the chef who went to work even if she was on death's door.

"She might have been seeing someone, she might have been going on dates we necessarily didn't know about but really, it was a non-thing as far as we were concerned.

"She wasn't exclusive with anyone at the time. She wasn't married or had kids to look after, she was just living her life - and why not?"

The allegations about their daughter's love life were a surprise to her parents.

Joan was furious and dismissed Mr Galloway's comments. Peter thought them insensitive but conceded he wouldn't have expected to know every detail of his daughter's private life.

"It was obviously difficult to hear and of course the media just went crazy with it," he says. "But she was a 35-year-old single woman, it would have been more unusual if she hadn't [had relationships]."

The investigation on the whole appeared to be hampered by a reluctant public wary of being implicated in what had been portrayed as a lurid scandal.

"The challenge is that you have to get people to come forward with information," reflects Mr Driscoll. "But that was hindered because of how the case was handled."

By the time Det Supt Dai Malyn had completed his review of the Claudia Lawrence case for North Yorkshire Police, he had reached a far blunter conclusion.

"I still strongly favour the theory that the person - or persons - responsible for Claudia's disappearance was someone - or several people - who were close to her.

"It was either very well-planned or there was a huge element of luck to have got away with it, so far at least.

"In my view they have probably been helped by the fact that those closely associated with Claudia have withheld key information."

The detective's comments in 2016 spoke to the frustration of a case which had left his force with a black mark in its unsolved crimes column for years.

https://www.bbc.co.uk/news/resources/idt-sh/what_happened_to_claudia

In my opinion, Ray Galloway's handling of this case shows us very clearly his personality traits. He is confrontational and does not listen to witnesses.

These facts, in my opinion, made him a wholly unsuitable person to lead the Speaking Out inquiry team.

The Speaking Out inquiry was set up to listen to and learn from victims and witnesses and would e handling testimony from them from up to sixty years ago.

These witnesses and victims had not been believed or had not felt they could come forward at the time because they would not be believed.

Witnesses from the staff of the hospital, who in some cases risked their careers by coming forward, as they were likely to be admitting to crimes of inaction, when they should have intervened, they were risking charges because of their testimony.

This inquiry needed sympathetic investigation, delicate handling, and careful listening by the team to stand any chance of success, but instead, they got Ray Galloway.

Chapter 12

CICA confirm victim status with compensation

More months elapsed, communications between myself and the ombudsman were scant, however I was building a picture that despite their claims to have to power to force the health service to cooperate, they did not have the level of control or powers they had claimed.

I was constantly reminded that my complaint was unique, that the ombudsman had never dealt with a complaint like mine and that everything they did was a first for them. They had never handled a complaint against the DOH, a government department, only having dealt with medical complaints against the NHS.

They did however state that they were prepared to take the DOH legal department to court to force their cooperation but warned that this would be in the high court, could take years, and could be subject to appeal.

At this point, CICA finally determined that I was a victim of sexual assault, this decision was based upon the police having recorded four crimes in my name.

In the absence of any prospect of compensation from the DOH or Savile's estate, I received a small payment.

I notified the ombudsman of this outcome as further proof that I was a victim of Savile, should they need more.

It Was Good While It Lasted

Chapter 13

Psychiatric care – at last

I had now completed forty-four meetings with the psychiatrist over the course of a year, sceptical at first, I was simply asked to talk for around fifty minutes about what had happened whist she listened. I did not take it seriously for several weeks, however by around seven weeks I ran out of story to tell, I was now spending time for several days before a meeting thinking of what to say in the next meeting.

Finally, the psychiatrist explained that we had reached a point she hoped we would, I was no longer thinking about the past, no longer writing notes in the middle of the night, and no longer losing so much sleep, she explained that she expected my treatment to take around forty-five meetings over a period of a year, and for the focus to reach a point where the only time I thought about the past horror stories, would be during the meetings with her.

She was right, the sleepless nights were getting to be a thing of the past, the thoughts now started to look to the future and my wife said I was a lot easier to live with.

After the completion of the meetings, I never now think about the past and how I could have changed the outcome with some action, or omission. I can recommend the course to anyone in my position, however as it is not normally available on the NHS, you may need to fight for a place.

It Was Good While It Lasted

Chapter 14

ombudsman second meeting year three

At the anniversary of the meeting with the ombudsman in Leeds, it was agreed that another meeting would be appropriate. I travelled with my friend to London to meet with the team in the ombudsman's headquarters in Millbank Tower, Westminster.

My MP Fabian Hamilton was present in the meeting and we started at 10:00 AM on Monday. First, the ombudsman's team and Fabian commented on how much better I looked, much more relaxed, I explained I had completed the course of psychiatric treatment and I was much better.

The ombudsman's team had an air to them we had not previously witnessed, they had, just the Friday before, received the documents from the DOH legal team, they had not had chance to fully scrutinise the documents or to check if they had received all the documents they had requested. However, they had read through these and now advised that.

1. The DOH was now cooperating with them.
2. They could not discuss the content as it was subject to client confidentiality.
3. They were now confident of concluding my complaint in a reasonable time Frome (this was the third year).

The team went on to give me hope that they were now considering the actions for the DOH and their reliance upon the meeting with the Speaking Out inquiry, a third party, to determine victim's civil liability claims.

They may now consider instructing the DOH to rerun the process, they did say however that the DOH legal team was threatening to sue the ombudsman through the courts depending upon the determinations they reached.

This statement led me, Fabian, and my colleague to believe that the ombudsman's report was likely to conclude soon and, in my favour, that if provided with the opportunity, and support in a second meeting to determine my victim status, this would be a very different meeting and may overturn the original decision.

Fabian then spoke on my behalf; he outlined his outrage at the way in which I had been misled into attending a meeting, then mistreated by the Speaking Out inquiry, who had failed to record large parts. and subsequently my claim had been denied by the DOH.

He advised the ombudsman that he had been a politician for longer than most and was adept at reading people in his surgery, he went on to say that he thought he could spot someone who was not telling the truth, and assured the ombudsman's team that in his opinion, I was completely truthful and that he believed my story entirely, he was assured I had been a genuine victim of Savile as a child.

I took the opportunity to thank the team for their difficult and complex work to date un bringing the DOH to a point of cooperation and persuading the DOH legal team to release the documents they needed.

However, after the meeting my colleague had his reservations, he noticed several issues with the ombudsman's team and their behaviour in the meeting, it was his opinion that their statement regarding legal action expected over their determination was of concern.

It was already in the public domain that the DOH had spent a vast sum on lawyers to defend the NHS against claims by Savile victims, this had reduced the number receiving compensation from hundreds down to tens, and he suspected that, should the ombudsman endeavour to force the DOH to rerun the meeting process, that this would re-open the flood gates of victims they had denied.

He believed this was why the ombudsman was threatened with high court action, to focus the ombudsman on the possibility of an awfully expensive legal battle in high court to prevent that can of worms being opened, and the inevitable extra cost, not to mention the loss of faith from the public in the process.

Months passed with no real communication from the ombudsman.

It Was Good While It Lasted

Chapter 15

DOH pays more in legal fees than compensation

The newspapers including the Times and the sun newspaper ran articles detailing the NHS/DOH payments to the victims of the Savile scandal; -

The NHS has been left with a £1m bill for compensating victims of Jimmy Savile after the late sexual predator's estate contributed just £53,000.

The DJ and television presenter raped and assaulted scores of patients, staff and visitors in 41 hospitals, a children's home and a hospice over nearly 50 years. Victims included children as young as five, paralysed teenagers in wheelchairs and pregnant women. Savile died aged 84 in 2011 before his crimes were revealed, and was reported to have had an estate worth at least £4m.

Of the £1.1m NHS bill, much of which is legal fees rather than compensation, Savile's estate paid £53,245, The Sunday Times can reveal. On average, 52 victims received just £9,615.

However, an independent inquiry found that the number of victims could have been as high as 177.

Sexual abuse survivors' groups branded the reimbursement from Savile's estate "pretty appalling" and described the payouts as "utterly derisory" and "peanuts".

Many of Savile's victims needed significant amounts of money to pay for private therapy that the NHS was often unable to provide, experts said. Some will require specialist care for the rest of their lives.

Peter Saunders, founder of the National Association for People Abused in Childhood, said: "The real winners in these situations tend to be the lawyers, I'm afraid."

About £600,000 of the £1.1m cost to the NHS went on legal fees, with the remaining £500,000 paid in damages to the 52, according to data released under freedom of information laws.

Saunders said it was "fundamentally wrong" that celebrities can get "a massive court settlement of damages" for being defamed, while Savile's victims ended up with an average of under £10,000 each after being sexually assaulted.

NHS Resolution, the body that handles negligence claims against the health service, confirmed that it had not been fully refunded by the TV presenter's estate. It said: "NHS Resolution was reimbursed £53,245.05 from Jimmy Savile's estate." Eight years after his death, the NHS is still dealing with a handful of "open cases", it added.

The revelations raise fresh questions over precisely what happened to Savile's wealth after he died.

The law firm Osborne Clarke received £1.2m for its work for NatWest bank, the estate's executor. Osborne Clarke said the fees were related to the processing of genuine claims made against Savile's estate as well as "other aspects of administration such as investigating a large number of false claims".

Richard Scorer, head of the abuse team at the law firm Slater and Gordon, which represented some of Savile's victims, said: "Ensuring that victims have proper access to therapy is a major issue — it's a constant problem that victims come up against. So when victims seek compensation, a big reason for doing that is because they want to have therapy, and the only way they can do that is privately."

The Department of Health said settlements for Savile's victims were negotiated between lawyers for the defendants and victims, and then approved in the High Court.

https://www.thetimes.co.uk/article/nhs-pays-over-1m-for-jimmy-saviles-sex-abuse-jqjlvmg36

'DERISORY & PATHETIC' Jimmy Savile victims given LESS in compensation than the NHS spent in legal costs

SHOCK figures reveal that the 52 patients abused in hospitals by Jimmy Savile were handed less in compensation than the NHS paid out in legal fees

The 52 victims of the pervert DJ received £500,000 in total — an average of just £9,615 each. But the NHS paid £600,000 in legal costs, including £110,000 on defending claims.

The figures, revealed to The Sun on Sunday in a Freedom of Information request, shows for the first time how meagre the full compensation package was.

Peter Saunders, founder of the National Association for People Abused in Childhood, described the payouts as "derisory".

He said: "The amount is pathetic, especially when you consider the NHS has spent more on lawyers.

"Why couldn't the NHS have avoided hundreds of thousands in legal costs by taking statements with the help of psychologists and agreeing reasonable payouts?

"The figures victims have received are derisory because it would cost a lot more to pay for the professional therapy they may need which is often not available on the NHS."

Many of the victims got compensation lower than £9,000 as three of those abused by Savile were awarded £40,000 each.

https://www.thesun.co.uk/news/8083278/patients-abused-jimmy-savile-compensation-nhs-paid/

These articles made it clear why the NHS/DOH had not wanted to cooperate with the ombudsman, in their opinion they had closed the can of worms called Jimmy Savile and did not under any circumstances wish to re-open it.

By ambushing victims in the Speaking Out interviews rather than listening to them, the NHS/DOH had reduced the number of 'victims' to 52 from a potential 177, a saving of £1.25Million at an average of £10,000 per victim.

More time passed and I chased up the ombudsman for an update, surprise, more complications had arisen with the DOH legal team, they were still withholding one document required by the ombudsman, however they were expecting this soon.

I then received an email. it was now determined that the ombudsman would require my entire file, this was agreed, and Liz Dux company released all documents in my case to the ombudsman.

More months passed, and eventually the ombudsman had reached a determination in my case. They wanted to set up a telephone call.

Chapter 16

The ombudsman's decision

At long last some four years after I filed a claim with the ombudsman, they wanted to hold a telephone call with me to explain their decision, and later wrote to me with the formal outcome.

It basically said that the NHS/DOH actions in utilising a third party, Kate Lampard, to manage the inquiry and interview the victims, fell outside the scope of the ombudsman.

It found that the DOH had erred in one of their communications, this had given me hope that I could overturn the outcome of their decision process and this was incorrect.

They awarded £500.00 in compensation for the error in communication which had given false hope.

My colleague was not surprised, it turns out that the Parliamentary and Health Service Ombudsman, did not after all have the powers to fully investigate the actions of the NHS/DOH in handling the largest abuse scandal the UK has ever known.

My MP Fabian Hamilton now dropped the case and never communicated with me about the outcome.

The threat by the DOH to take the ombudsman to court, had been taken seriously, and I would be denied justice and victim status as a result.

I wrote to the Ombudsman to say that I felt that £500 was far too great a sum for the minor clerical error they had uncovered, I suggested that £10 would be more appropriate.

I suspected that the DOH would once again forget my request for all communication by email, and that they would post me a cheque, this would have given me a chance for one final complaint. However, they emailed asking for a bank account to make the payment, so I did not reply.

I can now say with certainty, that between the legal teams on the ombudsman's side, and the lawyers on the DOH side, they must have spent hundreds of billable hours trying to avoid communicating, and when that failed, many more hours threatening each other.

The combined bill must have been at least twenty times the sum that I would have received in compensation, had they just accepted I was a victim.

Furthermore, it had always been my intention to give any compensation I may receive to charity, so ultimately the charities were the biggest losers in this sorry matter.

Chapter 17

File sent to IICSA

I told the ombudsman in my first meeting with them that I intended to file my story, along with the supporting documents with IICSA the Independent Inquiry into Child Sexual Abuse.

I was good to my word and shared all documents with them along with a letter for their attention, in my letter I describe the way I feel I have been played by the NHS inquiry and their legal department.

It is my belief that I am the only victim to actually witness Savile assault a dead body, that they wanted to shut me up and close my case down as my testimony was beyond what they could handle. I was never going to fit neatly into their published report. The scandal was just too great.

My letter to IICSA contained a small table; -

Those who believed I was a victim	Those who do not.
West Yorkshire Police	Ray Galloway
The Met Police	
My sister	
My solicitor	
CICA	
My GP	
My Psychiatrist	
My MP	
My MP's secretary	
My friend and confidant	
The Parliamentary Ombudsman	
IICSA	

Unfortunately, the one person who I met in person to discuss my abuse by Savile who did not believe I was a victim, was the one person the Speaking Out inquiry chose to determine witness's civil liability on behalf of the DOH.

My letter to IICSA concluded with advice I would now give to any person who has suffered historical sexual abuse.

Do not under any circumstances come forward and report it, as the fact remains true today as always, it is highly likely that you will not be believed.

The trauma and relief of finally telling your story is palpable, but when you are not believed, it is in my opinion further abuse and far worse than the abuse suffered originally.

Other than an acknowledgment in 2018 that IICSA have my contact details, they have not done so, I presume that as they require no further information, or to meet me to discuss this case of abuse, that they are happy with the way I have been treated.

As a victim of historical abuse, it was my opinion that IICSA were looking to right such cases and restore justice to those denied it.

Once again, I was proven wrong.

Chapter 18

Jeremy Hunt MP Statement

Jeremy Hunt MP, the Health Secretary said in the house; -

"Today I want to apologise on behalf of the Government and the NHS to all the victims who were abused by Savile in NHS-run institutions.

We let them down badly and however long ago it may have been, many of them are still reliving the pain they went through.

If we cannot undo the past, I hope that honesty and transparency about what happened can at least alleviate some of the suffering, it's the least we owe them.

Savile repeatedly exploited the trust of a nation for his own vile purposes and that victims who spoke up were not believed. He stressed it was important to recognise the profoundly uncomfortable truth of what the victims went through. I know this House, indeed the whole country, will share a deep sense of revulsion at what they (the investigations) revealed.

A litany of disturbing accounts of rape and sexual abuse committed by Savile on vulnerable children and adults over a period of decades.

At the time the victims who spoke up were not believed and it's important today that we all publicly recognise the truth of what they have said.

But it is a profoundly uncomfortable truth.

Savile was a manipulative, arrogant and controlling sexual predator who exerted an incredible level of influence and power within these hospitals.

But it's clear from these chilling reports that a culture of turning a blind eye to Savile's abuse of children was almost endemic among some staff at Leeds General Infirmary and Broadmoor hospital.

When victims spoke up or staff raised concerns they were dismissed out of hand, allowing Savile to operate in a perverse personal fiefdom within these institutions. It's hard to believe senior staff could be so blind to what was happening at ward level. And we need to question further how much senior staff actually knew and why they allowed a culture where abuse was ignored to exist.

Savile escaped justice because people didn't want to hear or believe what children were saying. Ministers now need to be satisfied that this could never happen again and that children and vulnerable adults in hospitals or any government facility are safe today."

Chapter 19

Missed opportunity

It is a shame that the NHS/DOH made the decision to outsource the inquiry and install a man like Ray Galloway.

By hijacking the meetings held under the guise of listening to the victims and witnesses. In order to learn from the past and prevent the same situation ever re occurring. The DOH denied compensation and or psychiatric care to most of those brave enough to come forward.

Using the meetings to determine civil and or criminal liability, despite this being beyond the scope of the inquiry, has doubtless put victims and witnesses off *speaking out*.

Had they taken a more magnanimous stance and done what the health secretary told them to do when he said, "the victims must be believed", they may have wasted a few thousand pounds on a handful of chancers but could have saved hundreds of thousands on legal fees.

In addition, only a few years later. Despite Jeremy Hunt's speech, we read once again in the press that another "Savile" style abuse scandal has been running for decades,

Maybe if they had listened during the Speaking Out meetings, rather than upsetting victims, others may have come forward. As a result, they may have detected the following crimes years sooner, in my opinion, those in authority, even cabinet ministers, may make great speeches, but they do not mean them.

The Daily Mail 25 November 2020

Porter at Great Ormond Street children's hospital, 55, is charged with 'decades-long catalogue of sex crimes against young boys he groomed at work'

Paul Farrell, 55, from Camden, north London worked at GOSH since the mid 80s

The porter was sacked after he was arrested by the Met Police in January 2020

He is expected to appear at Wood Green Crown Court in London on Friday

A porter at a world famous NHS children's hospital is appearing in court tomorrow morning having been charged with sexually abusing numerous children over the course of more than three decades.

Paul Farrell, 55, was arrested by the Metropolitan Police in January, having been accused of grooming children he met though his work at Great Ormond Street Hospital before sexually abusing them.

Farrell, who began working at GOSH in the 1980s is facing 84 charges, including sexually assaulting children, indecent assault on a male, attempted rape and rape.

He was also charged with paying for the sexual services of a child and making indecent photographs of a child.

Farrell, who is from Camden, north London, was sacked as soon as the allegations against him were made.

A spokesperson for Great Ormond Street Hospital told MailOnline: These are truly awful charges and we know that our hospital community, including our patient families, will have concerns or questions.

Due to the ongoing legal proceedings, we cannot go into the details of the case, but we can confirm that the individual who has been charged was dismissed from the Trust and we are continuing to work closely with the police.

Safeguarding children is fundamental to the care we provide. Our policies are in line with national best practice and include swift processes for managing concerns about staff when they are raised.

If anyone is concerned by what they have read in the media, the NSPCC have a helpline available on 0800 101 996 or email help@nspcc.org.uk.

As this is an ongoing police investigation, we are not able to say anything further at this current time for legal reasons.'

A Scotland Yard spokesman told MailOnline Farrell was arrested in January 2020 and has been charged with a total of 84 offences.

According to Scotland Yard: 'The charges relate to seven victims, and alleged offences committed between 1985 and 2018.

He is in custody, and is next due to appear at Wood Green Crown Court on Friday, 27 November for a plea and directions hearing.

Farrell was arrested on January 16, 2020, and first appeared at Highbury Corner Magistrates' Court upon charge. The ongoing investigation is being led by officers from the Central North Command Unit safeguarding team.'

Paul Farrell, 55, from Camden, is charged with the following offences (84 in total)

- Two counts of indecency with a child
- Twenty eight counts of indecent assault on a male
- Twenty counts of sexual assault of a child under 13
- Five counts of causing a child under 13 to engage in sexual activity
- Four counts of sexual activity with a child under 13
- One count of attempted rape of a child under 13
- Nine counts of sexual activity with a child under 16
- Three counts of causing a child under 16 to engage in sexual activity
- Two counts of attempted rape
- One count of rape
- One count of paying for sexual services of a child
- Three counts of possessing indecent photograph / pseudo-photo of a child
- Four counts of making indecent photograph / pseudo-photograph of a child
- One counts of possessing extreme pornographic images

https://www.dailymail.co.uk/news/article-8987481/Great-Ormond-St-porter-charged-child-sex-abuse-offences.html

End

I hope you found this autobiography informative, however I hope that the people and organisations described, most of whom failed to deliver when called to do so, can take heed and learn from my published experiences, remember I was just 12 years old when I met Savile.

Printed in Great Britain
by Amazon